Message from the Commissioner

The U.S. Customs and Border Protection (CBP), Air and Marine Operations (AMO) Vision 2025 represents the dedication and hard work of many personnel around the country to shape the future of AMO and its role in the homeland security mission.

CBP has a diverse mission to protect the American people from a variety of threats in multiple environments. In particular, AMO performs a unique role in securing our air and maritime environment, at the border and beyond. I applaud AMO's efforts and, as Commissioner, I'm proud of the work its people do every day in service to this great nation.

R. Gil Kerlikowske
Commissioner
U.S. Customs and Border Protection

Message from the Executive Assistant Commissioner

I am pleased to bring you the Air and Marine Operations Vision 2025.

AMO possesses a unique combination of authorities, capabilities, and agents and officers with expertise in the air and maritime environments. Simply put, no other agency in the federal government does what we do. AMO's 1,616 personnel are responsible for the operation and management of 257 manned and unmanned aircraft, 286 vessels, and a sophisticated domain awareness network. It is critical that such a technical, diverse, and widely dispersed force be brought to bear against our nation's threats in an efficient and effective manner.

This document provides our personnel with overarching guidance to counter the threats we face as a nation, outlines our primary core competencies, and establishes goals and objectives to successfully achieve our vision. These objectives are not all-inclusive; instead they represent the most critical steps we must take as we prepare for the future.

AMO Vision 2025 was developed to support the goals and objectives described in CBP Vision and Strategy 2020, DHS 2014-2018 Strategic Plan, and the DHS Southern Border and Approaches Campaign Plan. In particular, it highlights the importance of operating proactively to meet evolving threats, with increased emphasis on intelligence, investigations, and interagency partnerships, as well as continued coordinated operations within CBP. I am confident that it will spark a heightened sense of mission ownership among our entire workforce.

In summary, this plan provides AMO with a single unified strategy around which we will develop our policies, deploy our resources, conduct our training, acquire and maintain our fleet of aircraft and vessels, and execute our operations. It reflects my commitment to the people of AMO, to the mission of CBP and DHS, and to the security of the nation.

R. D. Alles

Randolph D. Alles
Executive Assistant Commissioner
Air and Marine Operations

Air and Marine Operations Vision 2025

Table of Contents

I. Mission and Vision

Mission

We are a federal law enforcement organization dedicated to serving and protecting the American people. We apply advanced aeronautical and maritime capabilities and employ our unique skill sets to preserve America's security interests.

Vision

Air and Marine Operations serves as the nation's experts in airborne and maritime law enforcement. We provide maximum benefit to the American people through our core competencies of *interdiction*, *investigation*, *domain awareness*, and *contingency operations and national taskings*.

We will hold ourselves accountable for success and ensure positive outcomes by pursuing the following overarching priorities.

Invest in Our People

Our people set us apart. Upon initial entry on duty, every AMO agent – at a minimum – is required to possess depth and expertise in the complex disciplines of maritime and/or aeronautical operations. We will provide training of the highest caliber while also broadening opportunities for diverse education and experience to better develop our future leaders. We train for our expected missions and prepare for the unexpected through education and experience.

Execute a Counter-Network Strategy

CBP's counter-network approach involves developing greater insight into terrorist and transnational criminal networks while working with our many partners to build a more cohesive community to disrupt and neutralize these networks. This approach establishes a collaborative initiative to detect, deter, disrupt, and neutralize terrorist and transnational criminal networks.

As an operational partner with numerous federal, state, and local entities, AMO is ideally positioned to participate in this counter-network strategy. We will apply advanced operational knowledge and expertise in the aviation and maritime environments and leverage our skill sets to lead and contribute to a flexible, whole-of-government counter-network strategy.

Develop and Sustain Our Fleet

AMO employs over 1,200 frontline agents. Despite this relatively small work force, we conduct our mission at the air, maritime, and land borders; the littoral, source, and transit zone approaches to the United States; and throughout the interior of the country. A capable and ready fleet of aircraft and vessels allows us the agility to succeed over such a large area. We will continually assess our challenges, and maintain the appropriate capabilities and equipment required for success. We must deploy advanced, effective technology, while aggressively pursuing opportunities for efficiency and commonality; well-planned sustainment of our fleet and mission systems is essential.

Build Our Domain Awareness

Domain awareness is one of our most critical contributions to securing the nation's borders and combatting criminal organizations. AMO will share real-time, actionable information by linking a vast network of sensors and sensor-equipped aircraft and vessels through a thoroughly modernized Air and Marine Operations Center (AMOC). By 2025, we will have developed and integrated one of the world's most advanced domain awareness and information networks, enabling rapid, informed decision-making by operators and commanders in the field.

Our mission, vision, and priorities form the basis of our plan for the next decade. In the following pages, we discuss our core competencies in greater detail. Finally, we outline goals and objectives to meet the evolving threat and achieve our vision in service of the American people.

II. Core Competencies

Over the past 10 years, AMO has largely concentrated its efforts and resources toward interdiction. This focus has been quite effective in high-threat areas with overt smuggling or illegal migrant activity. It has proven to be less effective when we are confronted with sophisticated organizations that capably employ deception, concealment, or emerging technologies. In the coming years, we will renew emphasis on the mission areas that enhance our awareness of criminal networks, and put us in the best position to disrupt their activities and organizations. These include investigation and domain awareness. We also recognize that AMO's critical role in emerging national taskings is growing and must be specifically planned for and resourced.

Thus, AMO's mission falls into four broad categories that reflect our core competencies: interdiction, investigation, domain awareness, and contingency operations and national taskings. These competencies are interdependent and mutually supporting. Success in one significantly contributes to success in all.

A. Interdiction

Interdiction encompasses our efforts to intercept, apprehend, or disrupt threats in the land, sea, and air domains as they move toward or across the borders of the United States. We

accomplish this through patrol activities, investigation, intelligence collection and analysis, and specifically targeted missions in response to actionable information. The importance of actionable information cannot be overstated. It is a critical factor for successful interdictions. Much of our organizational effort must be directed toward generating and exploiting it.

Beyond the Border

We are part of America's first line of defense against terrorists and their weapons, illegal aliens, and illegal drugs. In keeping with DHS and CBP strategy, our aim is to extend the U.S. zone of security well away from its borders. To accomplish this, we forward-deploy our P-3 aircraft and unmanned aircraft systems (UAS) in order to interdict threats as close to their source as possible. We conduct some of our most productive interdiction operations in the source and transit zones. For example, AMO's participation in Joint

Interagency Task Force South operations accounts for a large majority of the cocaine CBP seizes each year. When bulk shipments are not seized or disrupted in the source and transit zones,

they are typically split into smaller parcels for entry into the United States. These parcels are far more difficult to interdict, as evidenced by lesser amounts of cocaine seized at and between ports of entry. For this reason, we will continue to emphasize operations in the source and transit zones.

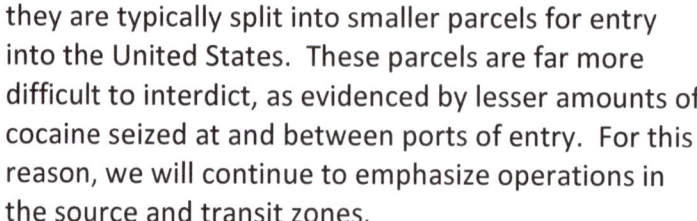

We will also increase using the above assets and others, such as our DHC-8 aircraft, to provide direct assistance to partner nations. In particular, we will continue our support to the government of Mexico, which has demonstrated improved ability to combat illicit flows and associated violence.

Succeeding in these endeavors will require sufficient numbers of skilled, deployable crews; reliable aircraft and mission systems; and flexible, responsive maintenance in the forward operating environment.

At the Border

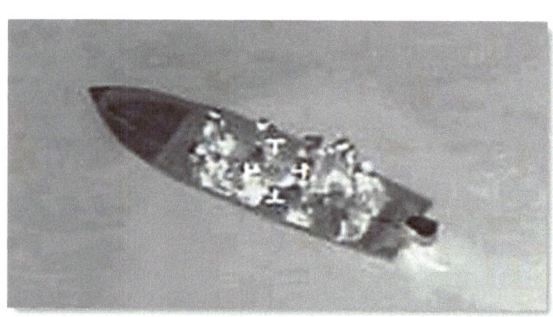

Despite our best efforts to extend the zone of security, threats will continue to arrive at our borders. Accordingly, much of our interdiction effort will occur in the border environment. In the land domain, we will continue to work in close partnership with U.S. Border Patrol, as well as other federal, state, local, and tribal partners. Reconnaissance, Surveillance, and Target Acquisition (RSTA) missions employing observation aircraft such as the UAS, PC-12, and C-206, as well as direct apprehension support to agents on the ground, are critical elements of our interdiction operations at our land borders.

As the C-206, PC-12 and other aircraft age, AMO will replace them with aircraft capable of carrying multi-sensor packages. We will also seek to expand operations and capabilities of the UAS, through increased availability and continued employment of advanced sensors such as ground moving target radar.

Light enforcement helicopters and medium lift helicopters will remain the eyes and legs of our land interdiction efforts. In the coming decade, we will move toward a more consolidated, agile aircraft fleet by reducing aircraft types while ensuring a robust capacity in terms of number of airframes and their capability.

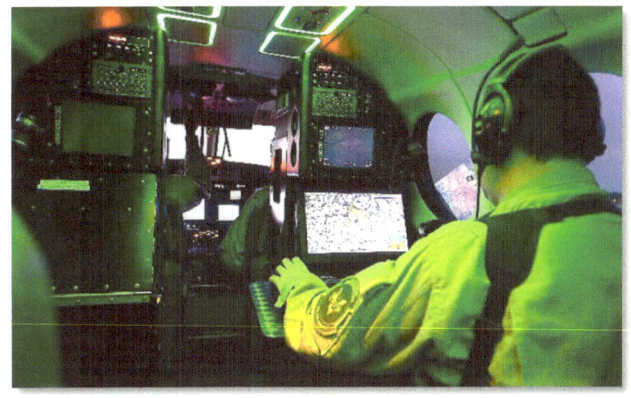

Increased interdiction presence at land borders has resulted in increased employment of maritime smuggling by transnational criminal organizations (TCOs). Accordingly, RSTA missions will remain a requirement at our sea borders, involving both AMO vessels and aircraft. Here, our interceptor vessels serve as apprehension platforms, either operating independently or with our maritime patrol aircraft (e.g., DHC-8 and Multi-Role Enforcement Aircraft) serving as the search/detection platform. We will continue to emphasize the latter combination, as it greatly increases the effective interdiction range of our vessels. We will upgrade our DHC-8 fleet with a new operating system and sensors in order to maximize this capability. As in the land domain, we will collaborate extensively with our maritime law enforcement partners, including the U.S. Coast Guard as well as other federal, state, and local entities.

Smugglers have employed increasingly circuitous routes to avoid detection by AMO and U.S. Coast Guard interceptors. Panga vessel landings occur ever farther north along the California coastline, while bales of cocaine and marijuana frequently wash up on remote Texas and Louisiana beaches, outside the operating footprint of

our maritime assets. New and shifting threat vectors like these underscore the need for increased strategic agility. We must enhance our ability to deploy manpower and assets based on risk. This may entail new permanent or temporary operating locations.

The makeup of our maritime fleet will be driven by mission requirements. Vessel types will include interceptors, platform vessels, and unmarked boats typical of their operating areas. To ensure an extended range of operations, we will deploy our next generation Coastal Interceptor Vessel (CIV). It will feature superior performance, reliability, and advanced capabilities, such as reliable over-the-horizon voice and data communication with the AMOC, aircraft, and other CIVs.

Our air interdiction mission is in transition. We are shifting from what has historically been a reactive posture, responding to air incursions with jet interceptors, to a more proactive, investigative approach. We will apply our unparalleled expertise in the air environment to establish networks within the law enforcement and general aviation communities. Information gained from these sources will allow for risk-based targeting of suspicious operators and

vulnerable airfields. We also seek to extend our air interdiction reach beyond our borders, chiefly through enhanced partnerships with Mexico and Canada. Sharing Air and Marine Operations Surveillance System data and cooperative interdictions of "short landings" (events where aircraft fly contraband up to, but not across, the border) are successful examples of this strategy.

Different challenges require different solutions. In some operating environments, the threat is self-evident. River crossings, airspace intrusions, vessels navigating with lights out, etc. are well-known cues of potential criminal activity. Where there is a high volume of illegal traffic, the smuggler can often rely on preoccupied law enforcement and a degree of stealth. Law enforcement is outnumbered, and cannot be everywhere at once. In such areas, our challenge is often bringing sufficient manpower and assets to bear to match the volume of the threat. As these high-threat areas tend to migrate over time, strategic agility is paramount.

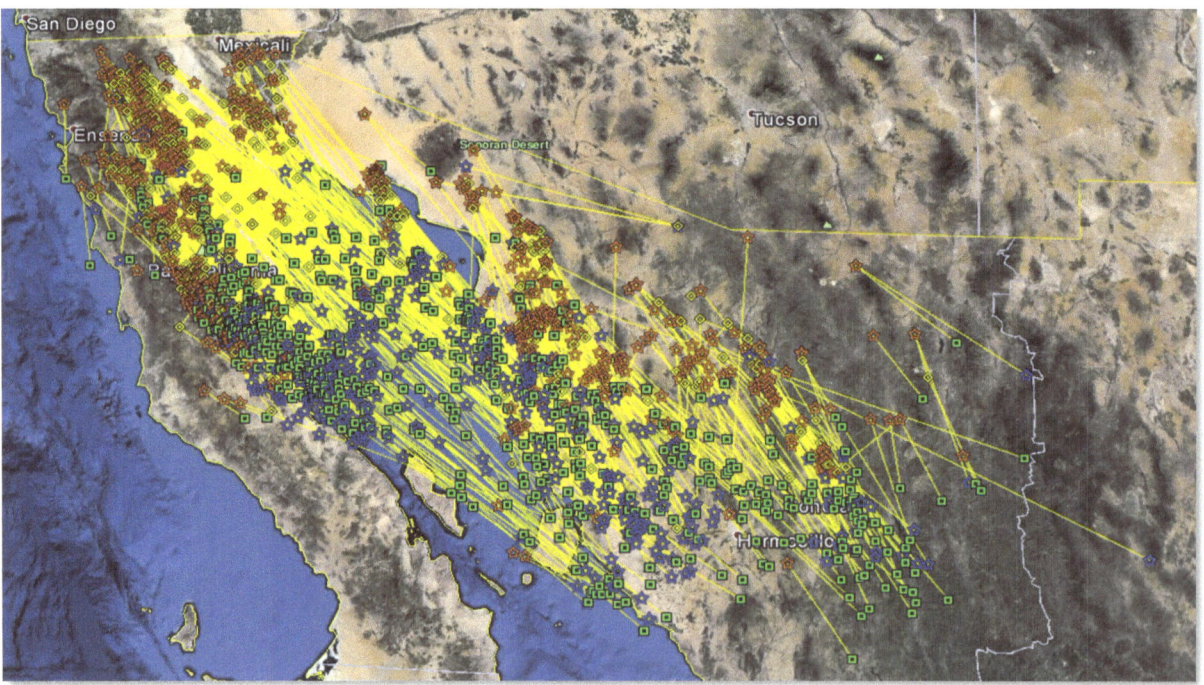

Figure 1. Short Landing Activity for Calendar Year 2014. Short landings are air smuggling events that land just south of the U.S. border. The figure identifies initial detection points, radar tracks, and the point where the contact fades from radar, for both the northbound and southbound (return) trip.

Other environments pose different challenges. Where there are high volumes of legitimate traffic near and across the border, threat profiles are less distinct and the smuggler can effectively comingle with normal traffic. This situation is particularly common in the maritime environment, where vessels enjoy freedom of movement through the U.S. maritime border from international and foreign waters.

Similarly, smugglers in the air environment often use the cover of normal air traffic and can be very difficult to identify. Increased situational awareness alone is insufficient to sort legitimate traffic from illegitimate in these areas; actionable intelligence is required to direct our efforts toward high probability targets.

In order to execute intelligence-driven operations, we will expand our investigative efforts and our participation in the intelligence enterprise.

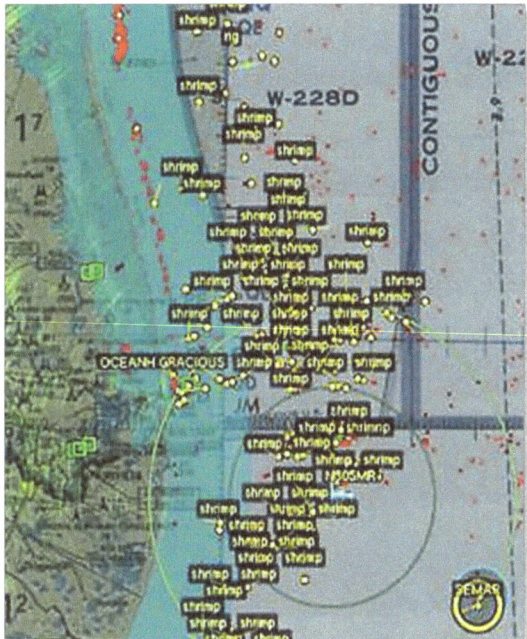

Figure 2. A DHC-8 sorts through numerous shrimp trawlers off the coast of South Texas and Mexico. Intelligence is required to differentiate between potential smugglers and vessels engaged in legitimate commerce.

GOAL 1 MAXIMIZE INTERDICTION EFFECTIVENESS

We must be increasingly agile in order to position the right people and assets in the right locations at the right times to effect interdictions. Operationally, that requires an ability to deploy quickly and flexibly. Strategically, we must conduct analyses to understand when and where our efforts yield maximum effect, and react decisively to those insights. Core to the success of our operations and our strategic decision-making is reliable intelligence.

OBJECTIVE 1.1 OPTIMIZE INTELLIGENCE-DRIVEN OPERATIONS

It is crucial that we employ our finite resources based on intelligence. Strategic and operational intelligence is essential to understand how an adversary conducts business. We will emphasize actionable, tactical intelligence to prevail against adaptive foes.

INITIATIVE 1.1.1 INCREASE PARTICIPATION IN THE INTELLIGENCE CYCLE

AMO will increase our participation in the intelligence cycle to derive maximum intelligence value from our operations. We will emphasize case and source development, leveraging our agents' unique expertise in the air and maritime environments. We will also integrate with national law enforcement and intelligence communities at the tactical, operational, and strategic levels. Specific steps include:

- Fully exploit seizures in partnership with investigative agencies
- Establish field intelligence liaison positions – increased communication with the Intelligence Community
- Expand AMOC's operational intelligence role and capabilities
- Outfit branch locations with appropriate equipment for classified communications (e.g., secure terminal equipment, Homeland Secure Data Network)
- Perform annual intelligence estimates
- Exchange personnel with intelligence offices and other agencies

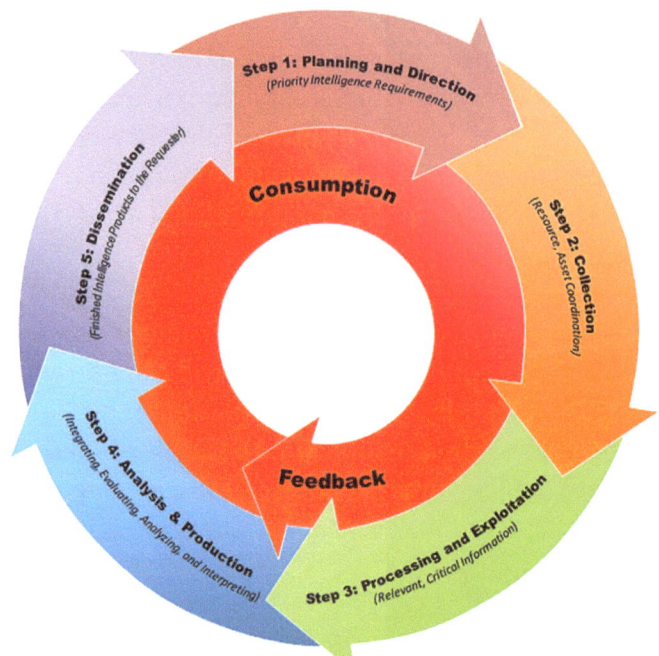

Figure 3. CBP Intelligence Cycle

OBJECTIVE 1.2 INCREASE STRATEGIC AGILITY

To respond effectively to rapidly changing threats, we must improve our ability to recognize and predict shifting trends and evolving tactics, techniques, and procedures of criminal organizations. We must have the ability to anticipate and plan for strategic shifts in threats, as well as the flexibility to respond to these shifts with risk-based decisions and timely redeployment of assets.

INITIATIVE 1.2.1 ENHANCE OPERATIONAL FLEXIBILITY

Enhance our ability to deploy personnel and assets in response to emerging or unanticipated threats and events, such as:

- Building sufficient capacity
- Programming for rapid surge capability (e.g., manpower, temporary duty assignment costs, premium pay)
- Seeking common platforms and training across common mission sets

Strategic agility requires us to continually align effectively against current and evolving threats. We will analyze threats and adjust our laydown and posture as appropriate. As threat vectors shift, we will deploy to temporary and permanent locations to support changes in mission requirements. National level analysis begins at AMO Headquarters, using statistical data analysis. Area analysis begins with the AMO leadership in the field, who are the subject matter experts for air and maritime domains within their respective areas of operation.

B. Investigation

At our core, we are a law enforcement organization. AMO is vested with primary authorities under U.S. Code Titles 8, 18, 19, 21, 31, 33, and 46, as well as numerous federal regulations. Accordingly, the nation requires us to enforce its laws, which range from criminal, to customs and immigration, and aviation and maritime laws and regulations. This responsibility is not confined to the border. It extends well beyond it, into the offshore environment; and well behind it, into the interior cities of the United States. We will renew emphasis on the full range of our law enforcement mission – particularly investigation, both independently and as members of partnerships, task forces, and other whole-of-government networks. AMO owns a critical role in defeating criminal networks, which begins with investigation. We possess skills uncommon or otherwise unavailable among law enforcement. Chief among these is the expertise of our agents in the air and maritime domains. We will pair our superior technical abilities with expertise in commerce, patterns of life, and anomalous behavior. Air and Marine agents should be familiar faces at fixed-based operators, marinas, commercial docks, and flight schools, and use these encounters as sources of information for criminal investigations.

As we expand our knowledge base and network of sources, we will use these gains to support our role as full partners in investigating criminal cases and applying information derived from them (e.g., interviews with high-interest suspects). We will engage our trained, experienced agents and officers; the tracking and analysis capabilities resident at the AMOC; our law enforcement technical collection (LETC) program; and a resurgent field intelligence capability to enhance all phases of criminal investigations. Our undercover program, human source development, electronic tracking, and a nascent electronic investigations program are additional specialized capabilities that we will bring to bear in this effort.

Participating in relevant task forces is an effective way to increase AMO's role in investigations. We will emphasize membership in Border Enforcement Security Teams (BEST), High Intensity Drug Trafficking Areas (HIDTA), Joint Terrorism Task Forces (JTTF), and other local and regional

task forces. As our manpower is limited, we will prioritize those task forces that are most actively engaged in case work relevant to our mission, or show the greatest potential for AMO to contribute substantially to public safety.

An investigative role where AMO has been notably successful is the covert surveillance and tracking of suspects by aircraft, vessel, vehicle, foot, or electronic means. This is a fundamental law enforcement capability that we will continue to develop and enhance. Working in partnership with U.S. Immigration and Customs Enforcement (ICE) Homeland Security Investigations (HSI), as well as many other federal, state, and local agencies, our expertise has proven critical to the successful disruption of TCOs within the United States and beyond. We anticipate steady growth for this mission, particularly in the urban and suburban environments. Where threat level dictates, we will permanently deploy personnel and assets to perform this mission more consistently and efficiently.

We will deploy our next generation of surveillance aircraft to conduct and support investigations. Future requirements will dictate whether these are manned, unmanned, or a combination of both. As we transition, we will maintain a robust covert surveillance capability and work to build capacity to satisfy mission requirements. As we develop new mission systems and communications equipment, we will ensure compatibility with our systems, networks, and evidentiary needs, as well as those of our law enforcement partners. Also, as surveillance technology continues to advance, so will privacy concerns. We will ensure that protecting civil rights and civil liberties is a primary consideration when acquiring new systems and developing doctrine for their use.

AMO is also tasked by regulation and policy with preventing the domestic movement of drugs, aliens, and other contraband via general aviation.[1] This is primarily an investigative responsibility. In the domestic realm, we operate under regulatory authorities and enforcement of U.S. criminal code, rather than border authority. Success here depends on proactive techniques such as source development and community engagement, rather than exclusively reacting to border incursions or performing certificate inspections. We will carefully engage trusted partners to assist with this mission. Thorough knowledge of the law and civil liberties as they apply to aviation are paramount to long-term success and viability. We must ensure our partners are well versed in these issues as well.

GOAL 2 ENHANCE INVESTIGATIVE EFFECTIVENESS

Through key associations with traditional partners such as ICE HSI and our own authorities, we will advance our role in performing effective criminal investigations. AMO will emphasize formal participation in task forces, as well as decentralized information gathering and networking by our enforcement and intelligence personnel. We must continue to bring the most advanced skills and tools to bear, and employ them where they can be most efficient.

OBJECTIVE 2.1 INCREASE INVESTIGATIVE CAPABILITIES

We will continue to develop specialized skills and capabilities that support investigations. Priorities include:

- Confidential human source development
- Case development and management
- Advanced surveillance techniques, video downlink, and distribution
- Cyber and technical collection
- Undercover operations
- Electronic tracking and monitoring

---

[1] CBP's requirement to track general aviation aircraft operating within the United States is codified in National Security Presidential Directive-47 (National Strategy for Aviation Security)/Homeland Security Presidential Directive-16 (Aviation Security Policy) and two supporting plans, the Air Domain Surveillance and Intelligence Integration Plan and the Aviation Operational Threat Response Plan. The Air Domain Surveillance and Intelligence Integration Plan specifically tasks CBP to detect and identify potential air threats to the United States. The Aviation Operational Threat Response Plan directs CBP to conduct "aviation law enforcement operations, including detecting, identifying, and interdicting potential air threats to national security, as well as investigative case support for prosecution of criminal law violations within its jurisdiction."

OBJECTIVE 2.2 PARTICIPATE IN TASK FORCES AND WHOLE-OF-GOVERNMENT NETWORKS

AMO is uniquely positioned to form or expand strategic partnerships with federal, state, local, and tribal agencies as a result of frequent joint operations. We will leverage this position to promote intelligence sharing across organizations. In keeping with CBP's counter network strategy, direct collaboration is encouraged at all organizational levels, particularly between agents, officers, and analysts of different agencies.

OBJECTIVE 2.3 ASSIGN SURVEILLANCE ASSETS TO HIGH THREAT AREAS

We anticipate a growing demand for covert airborne surveillance, particularly in urban and suburban environments. Many high-threat areas lie in and around interior cities of the United States, whereas the bulk of our manpower and assets are arrayed at or near borders. To more effectively and efficiently perform our surveillance missions, as well as operations with our federal, state, and local partners, we will coordinate locally to carry out extended operations in high-threat areas where transit time currently limits effectiveness. Each location will be appropriately sustained with dedicated air assets, personnel, and facilities to meet mission requirements.

C. Domain Awareness

Domain awareness is the observation of the operating domain (air, land, and maritime) and its baseline information. AMO will network sensors deployed on aircraft, vessels, and land-based persistent wide area surveillance systems (continuous sensor coverage over a fixed geographic area). This sensor network (observation) is combined with intelligence, law enforcement case work, and open source information to create domain awareness. Expanding our domain awareness helps to detect and understand anomalies, enabling situational awareness.

Situational awareness is the understanding of an event occurring or about to occur within a domain that could affect safety, security, the economy, or the environment. It is derived from domain awareness. Situational awareness provides meaning to all disparate events taking place throughout multiple domains. It also links events happening before and after an incident that can yield vital information which supports intelligence and/or investigative efforts.

Situational awareness supports timely, accurate, and informed decision-making. It enables field leadership to execute proactive law enforcement operations and puts operators in the right place at the right time. The AMOC is the central hub for domain/situational awareness.

Texas Gulf Coast - 2025

A DHC-8 aircraft on routine patrol detects and identifies numerous fishing vessels. As each vessel is identified by name and registration number, a mission sensor operator aboard the DHC-8 accesses AMO's domain awareness network to check law enforcement and open source databases, while simultaneously streaming video and sensor data of the vessel into the network.

AMOC is also observing the vessels over the network. An intelligence research specialist discovers a link between a particular vessel and a known TCO, and advises the aircrew, passing all relevant information via the network. A CIV (see photo at left) responds, relying on the same information to plot an intercept and plan a tactical approach. As the interceptor closes its range with the fishing vessel, it begins to contribute to the operating picture.

Meanwhile, a P-3 Airborne Early Warning (AEW) aircraft has been following a track of interest from the Caribbean into the Gulf of Mexico. A fully-networked common operating picture reveals that the air track is approaching the suspect vessel. An air interceptor launches and immediately begins using this same operating picture to calculate its intercept. The P-3 AEW assumes on-scene command and begins to de-conflict air traffic.

As the air track approaches the fishing vessel, it descends below normal land-based radar horizon, but the P-3 AEW and a coastal tethered aerostat radar system maintain contact. That data is seamlessly networked as all assets share an uninterrupted tactical picture.

From six miles away, the crew of the DHC-8 observes a single-engine airplane overfly the fishing vessel and drop several packages before continuing Northbound. As the fishing vessel retrieves the packages, the crew of the CIV sees this video in real-time and begins a final intercept.

The CIV stops the suspect vessel, seizes 45 bales of cocaine still in plain view, arrests the crew and seizes the vessel. The air interceptor continues to use radar data from the AEW to covertly follow the airplane into a municipal airport, detain the pilot, and eventually obtain a search warrant. A search of the airplane reveals an additional kilo of cocaine. Agents arrest the pilot, and seize the cocaine and airplane.

AMO's Domain Awareness Network is made up of:
- Sensor Systems
    - persistent wide area surveillance systems
    - sensor systems deployed on aircraft and vessels
- Law Enforcement Information
    - human sources
    - case information
    - analysis of adversary's response to operational TTPs
- Intelligence
    - Organic
    - Intelligence Community's family of intelligence systems and sources
- Open Source Information

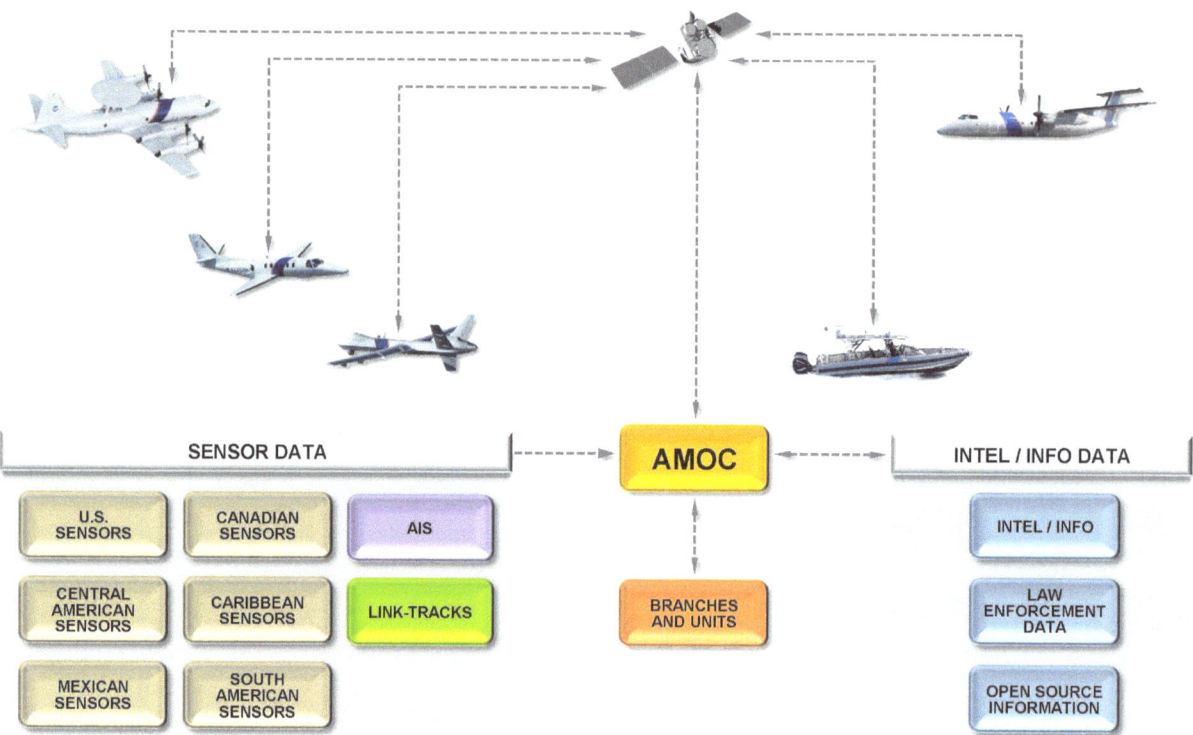

Figure 4. AMO's Domain Awareness Network. Aircraft and vessel crews, as well as operators at the AMOC will share sensor feeds, intelligence, and other vital information in real time, enabling coordinated planning and interdiction.

All data will be integrated and analyzed at the AMOC and then distributed through AMO's distribution systems.

Although awareness within the maritime and land domains is not as developed as in the air domain, we will pursue an operationally proactive concept to mature our capabilities within those domains.

OBJECTIVE 3.1 IDENTIFY AND ADVOCATE FOR SENSOR TECHNOLOGIES

AMO will explore new and emerging sensor technologies and develop an investment strategy to bring more capable and sustainable sensors to the field.

- Air Domain – We will identify, deploy, incorporate, and network additional foreign and domestic sensors.

- Maritime Domain – We will develop our maritime surveillance requirements in the coastal border regions and beyond. We will partner with maritime stakeholders for an adequate mix of technology and intelligence to create maritime situational awareness for a unified approach to global maritime security.

- Land Domain – We will work with other CBP offices and interagency partners to integrate ground domain awareness technology into the AMO domain awareness network. We will position ourselves to share these capabilities to advance ongoing and future efforts to improve land domain awareness.

OBJECTIVE 3.2 NETWORK EXISTING SENSOR SYSTEMS

AMO's multi-domain awareness network shall integrate multiple sensor technologies, intelligence and law enforcement databases, open source information, and extensive communications to create domain awareness and situational awareness. The network will be robust enough to add existing sensor feeds from all domains. The network will interface with existing CBP and DHS systems and share the data with other federal agencies as required.

AMO will network current and future persistent wide area surveillance systems with sensors deployed on aircraft, vessels, and the AMOC to ensure they share the same operational picture.

OBJECTIVE 3.3 ACCESS INTELLIGENCE AND OTHER INFORMATION

AMO will develop the ability to share intelligence and other information between all operational nodes within the AMO domain awareness network. The AMOC will have the ability to push/pull information to/from aircraft and vessel crews, and air and vessel crews will have the ability to access intelligence and information as needed.

AMO will continue to make incremental enhancements toward developing a network architecture that uses advanced technology, integrates classified and unclassified data, blends intelligence and other information, and increases sensor capacity while improving interoperability and compatibility with legacy systems. We will make sensor data, intelligence, and information available to partners to support their mission requirements.

D. Contingency Operations and National Taskings

In addition to its steady-state operations, AMO is mandated to perform a range of incident-based aviation and maritime missions, including a number of missions where AMO is designated as the primary operating organization.[2] Contingency operations and national taskings encompass the following missions:

- Federal Disaster Relief
- Continuity of Operations (COOP)
- Humanitarian Operations
- Terror Threats and Incidents
- Search and Rescue
- Special Events - National Special Security Events (NSSE) and Special Event Assessment Rating (SEAR)
- Radiation Detection and Monitoring
- Maritime and Port Security

---

[2] The authorities and source documents that mandate these AMO missions include, but are not limited to Department of Homeland Security Management Directive 0021, Aviation Concept of Operations; Department of Homeland Security Strategic Plan; DHS Air Surveillance Requirements; the National Interdiction Command and Control Plan; and the DHS Appropriations Act.

AMO has historically excelled at contingency and national tasking operations largely by applying organic capabilities developed for our interdiction, investigative, and domain awareness missions. Through experience, we have honed organization-wide skills, such as communications support, change detection, and video downlink, which are readily adapted to various exigencies. Increasingly, however, these

operations have become core to our mandate to serve and protect the American people. Accordingly, we have begun to refine skills specific to this mission, such as hoist rescue and the Air and Marine Emergency Medical Service.

In the coming years, we will continue to embrace our role as first responders and refine these unique operations. Utility for special missions will be an essential consideration as we develop operational requirements for platforms and systems. As appropriate, search and rescue techniques will be an integral part of our training for aircraft and vessels. We will emphasize interoperability with first responders such as U.S. Border Patrol Search, Trauma and Rescue (BORSTAR) and the U.S. Border Patrol Tactical Unit (BORTAC), and contingency partners such as the National Nuclear Security Administration, while strengthening AMO's own capabilities, such as airspace security, detection, and monitoring and interdiction response.

GOAL 4 PREPARE FOR CONTINGENCIES AND NATIONAL TASKINGS

Unlike our other core missions, AMO is not continually engaged in contingency operations and national taskings. To be effective when called upon, we must emphasize advanced capabilities, readiness, and training.

OBJECTIVE 4.1 MAXIMIZE READINESS AND TRAINING

AMO will identify core skills essential to contingency operations and national taskings, and ensure broad and recurring training. Some examples are below:

- Basic first aid
- Search and rescue
- Airspace security and intercepts
- Incident Command System expertise
- Helicopter Rope Suspension Techniques (HRST)
- Video downlink and distribution

OBJECTIVE 4.2 EXPAND CONTINGENCY CAPABILITIES

AMO will identify key present and future requirements for contingencies and national taskings through capability gap analysis. The ability to contribute to this mission set will be a significant factor for future acquisitions and program development.

E.   Sustain and Strengthen AMO

Success in our mission requires continued growth and development of our workforce, capabilities, and fleet. AMO will develop and select bold, dynamic leaders to drive high performance, foster innovation, and promote safety. We will renew emphasis on law enforcement core competencies, while continuing to refine our advanced technical skills.

New capabilities will be required to combat evolving threats. As disruptive technologies emerge at an accelerating rate, it is critical that we remain leaders in innovation. AMO will pursue technologies with significant law enforcement potential, both independently and in partnership with other organizations such as DHS Science and Technology. Examples of these technologies include remotely piloted aircraft and maritime platforms; sensors, such as space-based imagery technologies; and mission integration, communication, and data exploitation systems. However, we must also maintain sufficient resources by sustaining proven, reliable platforms and systems. It will be vital that we make efficient use of finite resources.

GOAL 5 CONTINUE AMO'S GROWTH AND DEVELOPMENT

We will pursue standardization and interoperability across our fleet, assets, and infrastructure. We must also ensure that our maintenance efforts align properly with operational requirements.

OBJECTIVE 5.1 SUPPORT WORKFORCE EXCELLENCE

Underwater egress training is part of the specialized instruction AMO aircrew complete to perform law enforcement in the air and maritime domains.

A well-trained, innovative, and committed workforce is essential to our success. Every employee must understand their role in accomplishing our mission and securing a safer homeland. We will take positive steps to reinforce our law enforcement culture while continuing to provide the highest quality education and training. We must also refine tools and processes so our force is correctly balanced to meet the threat as it evolves.

We will identify emerging leaders and provide them with the necessary range of experience and developmental tools to assume critical roles throughout the organization. Leaders must also vigilantly reinforce a strong and positive safety culture, which is fundamental to our aviation and maritime operations. To support all of the above, we will improve communication and collaboration, and remove barriers to innovation.

INITIATIVE 5.1.1 FORTIFY LAW ENFORCEMENT TRAINING AND CULTURE

We will reinforce our essential law enforcement values, from an employee's first contact with AMO, through field training, and throughout his or her career. We must also integrate our non-enforcement personnel into our law enforcement mission focus, sharing challenges and celebrating our successes together. Specific steps include:

- Enroll incoming agents in the best available law enforcement curriculum to include criminal investigative techniques
- Establish and maintain a standardized field training program for new agents and officers
- Promote physical fitness
- Establish a new employee orientation program to provide all incoming AMO employees with awareness and understanding of our mission
- Provide diverse developmental opportunities to law enforcement mission support personnel
- Maintain a robust Critical Incident Response Team

INITIATIVE 5.1.2 LEADERSHIP DEVELOPMENT AND SUCCESSION MANAGEMENT

AMO will build a strong leadership team through workforce development, performance management, and succession planning. We will promote an environment in which our frontline employees exercise leadership throughout the organization. We will reward and promote based on merit, leadership potential, and commitment to mission success. Leaders must acquire diverse experience and education, while amassing and retaining sufficient professional knowledge to command effectively. The following steps comprise AMO's succession management process:

- Identify key leadership positions
- Identify competencies, skills, and success factors of leadership
- Assess current bench strength
- Design and carry out career development strategies
- Monitor and evaluate strategies

INITIATIVE 5.1.3 DEVELOP A COMPREHENSIVE SAFETY PROGRAM

It is crucial that AMO maintain high safety standards as a foundation to operational excellence. In keeping with this philosophy and the fact that a robust safety program reduces mishaps, AMO will develop a safety management system committed to safety policies, risk management, safety assurance, and promotion. This will include:

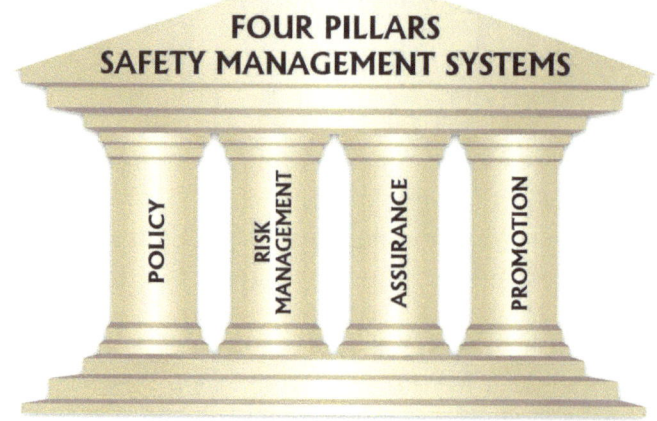

- Sound policies and procedures that reflect a commitment to improve safety
- Effective risk mitigation measures
- Safety assurance measures that validate the effectiveness of AMO safety programs
- Safety education and promotion

INITIATIVE 5.1.4 FOSTER INNOVATION AND ENGAGEMENT

AMO operates in a highly technical, evolving environment. We face threats that rely heavily on emerging technology and unconventional tactics. To counter these challenges, it is essential that we employ creativity and engagement throughout our own ranks. Some examples follow:

- Streamlined pilot programs for promising new techniques and technologies
- Improved internal communications and sharing of best practices through online tools and social media
- Increased recognition of high performers and innovators across the organization

INITIATIVE 5.1.5 ENSURE MISSION-APPROPRIATE MANNING LEVELS

AMO will develop a workforce staffing model that analyzes mission requirements, core and collateral duty assignments, required skill sets and technical expertise, and the necessary staffing mix that maintains AMO's capabilities at the highest level. The results will inform a bottom-up table of organization review process to ensure that manning levels are optimized to meet mission requirements, including both operational and support personnel.

OBJECTIVE 5.2 ACHIEVE AND MAINTAIN AN APPROPRIATE BALANCE OF FORCES

AMO will make risk-based, resource-informed procurement and sustainment decisions. These will be based on current and projected operational requirements, developed to support AMO's Vision 2025.

INITIATIVE 5.2.1 ESTABLISH A REQUIREMENTS MANAGEMENT PROCESS

Accurate allocation of resources based on requirements is necessary to fully engage the force against the threat. Requirements will be derived from risk-based, operational analysis. Specific steps include:

- Conduct bottom-up capability gap analyses
- Document consolidated requirements
- Effectively communicate requirements, objectives, and inherent risks to internal and external stakeholders

INITIATIVE 5.2.2 MEET EMERGING CAPABILITY REQUIREMENTS

Unique and diverse capabilities set AMO apart. We will continue to be a technology leader, while emphasizing sustainment and integration of proven systems. A highly educated and experienced program management and engineering staff is critical to this effort. Some present or emerging requirements include:

- Establish a fleet-wide strategy to modernize sensors, improve sustainability, and plan upgrade paths
- Modernize voice and data communications, including:
  - Interoperability with all federal, state, and local partners
  - Over-the-horizon communications for vessels
  - Hemispheric communications coverage between all platforms and AMOC
- Achieve universal networking of sensors, data, and voice between AMO aircraft, vessels, and the AMOC
- Deploy next generation of light surveillance aircraft (manned and/or unmanned) without disruption to required capacity
- Maintain an air-to-air intercept capability consistent with evolving mission requirements
- Develop and fully deploy a next-generation CIV
- Deploy non-standard vessels consistent with local maritime traffic for covert surveillance and undercover support
- Develop and integrate modern data and knowledge management systems to improve collaboration and accountability

INITIATIVE 5.2.3 PURSUE COMMONALITY

Disparate aircraft types provide a diverse array of capabilities, but frequently come at the cost of economy and commonality. We will seek opportunities to consolidate our aircraft fleet, while ensuring no degradation in mission readiness.

INITIATIVE 5.2.4 IMPLEMENT AN AVIATION AND VESSEL MAINTENANCE PLAN ALIGNED WITH OPERATIONAL REQUIREMENTS

In addition to modern capabilities, we must maintain sufficient capacity to meet mission requirements. To that end, we must strive to improve readiness and reduce the impact of maintenance as a limiting factor. Maintenance efforts and acquisitions will be tailored to achieve the following:

- Flexible, deployable, service-based maintenance
- An emphasis on mission capable aircraft, vessels, and systems. This will require a robust maintenance program, with technicians trained to repair highly complex radar, cameras, mission management systems, and avionics.
- A highly developed national logistics and maintenance staff
- A strong safety culture leading to reduced risk of maintenance-related mishaps

III. Conclusion

This Vision 2025 sets our direction and priorities for the coming years. In some cases it calls for significant change in our posture, outlook, or operations. Change is inevitably accompanied by some difficulty. It's important that we persevere and transform AMO to better prepare for the future.

Advancing technology and shifting threats will necessitate adapting our TTPs, often in ways we can't predict. However, we believe that our core competencies of interdiction, investigation, domain awareness, and contingencies and national taskings are enduring. To maintain and advance these competencies, we must continue to hire, train, and develop highly skilled employees and leaders. We must empower them with a sense of mission ownership and encourage them to explore new and innovative ways to succeed. We must remain on the leading edge of technology while simultaneously embracing our law enforcement roots and culture.

Despite often restrictive budgets and other challenges, AMO continues to adapt and succeed. In the coming years, we expect our role in protecting the American people and homeland to be more critical than ever. We are committed to success.

IV. Appendices

Appendix A: Methodology

The following sections outline the methods AMO used to assess its threats and document its core competencies, goals, initiatives, and implementation plans, as well as how it intends to implement and maintain the plan.

How the Vision Was Developed

AMO assembled planning teams to guide the development of the Vision 2025, accurately represent all stakeholders, account for diverse viewpoints, and integrate AMO's broad expertise.

- The Senior Guidance Team, comprised of AMO executive leadership, provided the mission and vision for the organization, as well as the overall direction of the strategic vision. Its members analyzed documents and presentations from the Headquarters and Field Planning Teams to guide the strategic planning process.

- The Field Planning Team was comprised of operators who provided subject matter expertise on threats, operating environment, and mission requirements. As a plan to achieve the organization's operational mission, the Field Planning Team led the development of the goals and objectives. Its members conducted extensive analysis of current threats and the operational environment using a risk-based approach and performance management techniques. This process generated the proposed goals, objectives, and initiatives to guide the next 10 years for the organization.

- The Headquarters Planning Team conducted extensive analysis through benchmarking and review of national and strategic plans. The members analyzed AMO goals, objectives, and initiatives, applying their expertise in identifying impacts and implementation guidance, which helped to refine the vision.

How the Vision Will Be Implemented

Directorates within AMO Headquarters implement the goals, objectives, and initiatives highlighted in the Vision 2025. On an annual basis, the strategic vision will guide AMO mission priority development, providing the basis for AMO's annual mission priorities submission to the Office of the Commissioner.

How the Vision Will Be Measured

AMO will establish measures to track progress toward achieving the specific goals and objectives of the Vision 2025. The results of these measures will be reported annually, and reviewed during AMO's Quarterly Management Reviews (QMRs). Through the reporting of performance measures and status updates during QMRs, AMO will track progress and identify when course corrections are necessary.

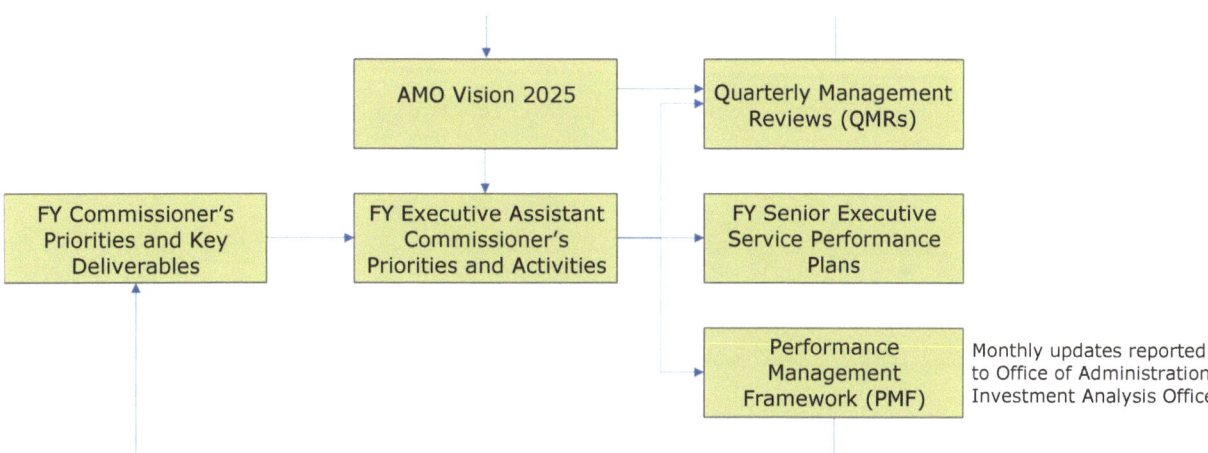

In addition, the goals and objectives included in AMO's annual mission priorities will be tracked in the Performance Management Framework, which utilizes a monthly reporting format. These goals and objectives will also form the basis of the performance plans of the Senior Executive Service personnel.

How the Vision Will Be Updated

AMO will formally update the Vision 2025 annually, based on a review of planning criteria and performance measure outputs. The document may be updated more frequently on an as-needed basis.

AMO monitored the development, reviewed drafts, and analyzed the 2015 releases of the CBP and DHS strategic plans, as well as the Southern Border and Approaches Campaign Plan. As a result, AMO ensured that its core competencies directly align with CBP goals, DHS missions, and the lines of effort of the Southern Border and Approaches Campaign Plan (see Appendix B).

AMO will continue to review DHS, CBP, and national strategic plans to maintain an awareness of changes in direction and requirements. AMO will also continue to benchmark relevant strategies and methodologies for strategic planning and evaluating programs and policies.

Appendix B: Core Competency Alignment

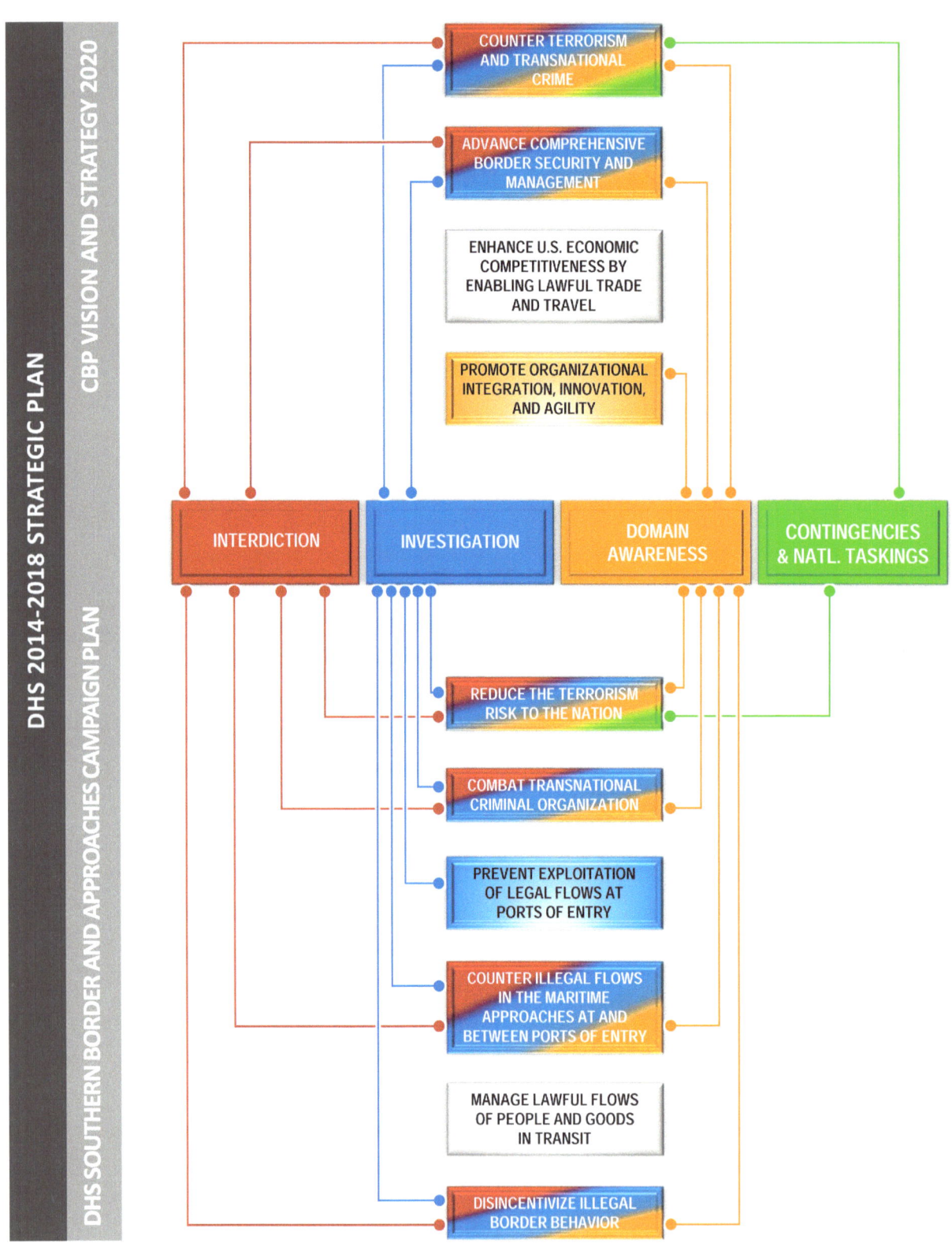

Appendix C: Bibliography

National Security Council. <u>Air Domain Surveillance and Intelligence Integration Plan</u>. March 26, 2007

National Security Council. <u>Aviation Operational Threat Response Plan</u>. March 26, 2007

National Security Council. <u>National Security Presidential Directive-47/Homeland Security Presidential Directive-16: National Strategy for Aviation Security</u>. March 26, 2007

Office of National Drug Control Policy. <u>The National Interdiction Command and Control Plan</u>. March 17, 2010

U.S. Customs and Border Protection. <u>Vision and Strategy 2020: U.S. Customs and Border Protection Strategic Plan</u>. 2015

U.S. Customs and Border Protection, Office of Office of Intelligence and Investigative Liaison. <u>Cocaine Semi-Annual Drug Report</u>. 2013

U.S. Customs and Border Protection, Office of Office of Intelligence and Investigative Liaison. <u>Heroin Semi-Annual Drug Report</u>. 2013

U.S. Customs and Border Protection, Office of Office of Intelligence and Investigative Liaison. <u>Increase of Cocaine Transshipped Through Puerto Rico and the Dominican Republic</u>. 2014

U.S. Customs and Border Protection, Office of Office of Intelligence and Investigative Liaison. <u>Marijuana Semi-Annual Drug Report</u>. 2013

U.S. Customs and Border Protection, Office of Office of Intelligence and Investigative Liaison. <u>Methamphetamine Semi-Annual Drug Report</u>. 2013

U.S. Customs and Border Protection, Office of Office of Intelligence and Investigative Liaison. <u>Mexico-United States Semi-Annual Border Joint Threat Assessment</u>. 2013

U.S. Department of Homeland Security. <u>Department of Homeland Security Campaign Plan for Securing the U.S. Southern Border and Approaches</u>. January 23, 2015

U.S. Department of Homeland Security. <u>Department of Homeland Security Management Directive 0021, Aviation Concept of Operations</u>. April 18, 2005

U.S. Department of Homeland Security. <u>DHS Air Surveillance Requirements.</u>

U.S. Department of Homeland Security. Strategic Plan for Fiscal Years 2014-2018. December 2014

U.S. Drug Enforcement Administration. National Drug Threat Assessment Summary. 2014

U.S. Drug Enforcement Administration. National Drug Threat Assessment. 2015

U.S. Department of Justice, National Drug Intelligence Center. Puerto Rico/U.S. Virgin Islands High Intensity Drug Trafficking Area Threat Assessment. 2014